D1391291

THIS IS A PARRAGON BOOK

© Parragon 1996

Parragon
13-17 Avonbridge Trading Estate
Atlantic Road, Avonmouth,
Bristol, BS11 9QD

Produced by The Templar Company plc,
Pippbrook Mill, London Road, Dorking
Surrey RH4 1JE

Designed by Mark Kingsley Monks

Printed and bound in Great Britain

ISBN 0 75252 064 4

THE
Jam Pandas'
FIRST BOOK OF
Counting

ILLUSTRATED BY STEPHANIE BOEY
WRITTEN BY CLAIRE STEEDEN

P
‖ · PARRAGON · ‖

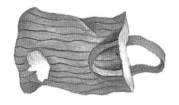

Big Bamboo has been to the shops to buy ten jars of jam.
But when he gets home his bag is empty.
Can you help him to find the ten jam jars?

One jam jar has
fallen by the doorstep.
Can you find it?
Big Bamboo picks it up
and puts it in his basket.

He has one jam jar.
Can you also find
one bird, one gate
and one dustbin?

1

One jam jar has rolled
into the long grass.
Can you find it?

Big Bamboo has
two jam jars.
Can you also see two
birds, two mice,
and two beetles?

One jam jar is in
the flower bed.
Can you find it?
Big Bamboo has
three jam jars.

Can you also see three butterflies, three bees and three flowers?

One jam jar has rolled
behind a tree.
Can you find it?
Big Bamboo has
four jam jars.

Can you also see four squirrels, four trees, and four fallen apples?

One jam jar is in the
strawberry patch.
Can you find it?

Big Bamboo has
five jam jars.
Can you find five
caterpillars, five
strawberries and five
flowerpots?

One jam jar is in the park.
Can you find it?
Big Bamboo has six
jam jars.

6

Can you also find six dogs,
six ducks and six tyre swings.

 1 **2** **3** **4** **5** **6**

One jam jar is by
the bus stop.
Can you find it?

Big Bamboo has seven
jam jars.

Can you see
seven birds, seven
umbrellas and
seven railings.

One jam jar has fallen
by a bicycle.
Can you find it?
Big Bamboo has eight
jam jars.

Can you find eight
pineapples, eight posters
and eight boxes?

One jam jar has rolled next to a lamppost. Can you find it?

Big Bamboo has nine jam jars.

Can you find nine leaves, nine lampposts and nine balloons?

9

One jam jar has
splashed into a puddle.
Now Big Bamboo has
all ten jam jars, so he
goes home again to
make a big blueberry
jam sandwich.

Can you see ten cones, ten footprints and ten puddles?

Titles in this series include: